FIRST LOOK

FIRST LOOK

—

Poems

JACQUELINE HENRY

OUTPOST PRESS
ABIQUIU, NEW MEXICO

"...after you survive the terrors
of the first look, and the long yearning at the window,
and that first walk —the one walk—together through the garden:
lovers, are you still the same?..."

—Rainier Maria Rilke, *Duino Elegies*

CONTENTS

AUTOBIOGRAPHY

When I was a child I'd sit
on the milk-box on the stoop
next to the screen door my
mother had locked after forcing

us out to play in the sun,
the shiny metal box hot
on my thighs as my sister's wet face
pressed into the screen where just

inside, the magical world we had forged
all morning lay in the dark coolness—
a sprawling kingdom beneath the sofas and
end tables and behind the thick chenille

curtains. And now, the child within me
grasps my pen and—oh so gently—
unlocks the screen door.

A I R

In fifth grade health class we were given
pieces of lung and a straw

and told to blow out not suck in
when for most of the decade
we had been living on this planet
we were taught about intake and not
about letting go, not about how
a long exhale could actually
inflate us.

One of the boys—of course
it was a boy, the girls were too careful
to inhale blood especially when
some of us had already begun
to bleed and were already
grossed out by this body, and
what it held—

well...   he sucked in.

Someone had to do it. Be funny.
Breakup the enormity of the
idea that this slab of tissue on
this table in front of us, this slab that
looked like raw meat on waxed
deli paper, had a function and

its function was life.

I forget who it was, one of the boys
who didn't want to listen
one of the ones I hung out with later
because I didn't want to listen—
because I just wanted to feel what
was inside of me—this great expanse of
unknowing, this thing pulsing within

me as we passed a bone between us
smoking in the field behind the school—
not remembering that I once held
something of myself in my hand
and felt its pulsing (does a dead
pig's lung pulse?) because that's what

I remember now, and this boy
grossly sucking in—

And everyone laughing but not wanting to
laugh, wanting to gag, and gagging then with
him, choking then with him and the teacher
rushing forward and this boy coughing up that
piece of pig's lung caught in his own lung
just because—yeah—he sucked in.

I don't know, maybe he wanted to know,

then at 10, what it would be like to slurp in a life
before his own deflated. Maybe he knew
what would happen to him later but didn't know how
to translate the years, didn't know that one day he'd be
cut down by the same sized straw, by the inhale

of something he thought would make his life
more livable when all he needed,

                all we ever needed
was to exhale the moment and deplete ourselves of
                        all that air.

BE STILL

I don't know what that means.
It's not even technically possible
with all this churning and chattering
inside of me; all these jumping quarks.

Be Still

meaning: stop the mind-itching, toe twitching,
fingers fingering—trying to figure out that
which is unfigurable—

Unknowable.
Lord, why make me observe it then?

Be Still

You want me to reach in
so I can reach out—
You want me to swan dive
into that pit
of loneliness and feel
how emptiness
fills me—You say,

Be Still and Know

That I am—

Enough.

FINDING ST. BARBARA, 2001

I found St. Barbara lying face down on
the pavement in the street sand by the curb
with the pebbles and the broken glass.

I nearly ran right over her,
a lightness in my steps,
but stopped short when I saw the coated

mass card, a little shimmer in the morning sun.

That I didn't trip over my own feet was itself
a miracle because it was a fast run day and
I was supposed to be timing myself. But

what is time when someone is lost?

This was someone somebody had thought enough to
carry—this patron saint of armory and explosions—but
not given enough thought to give the deceased a name, or

cite a date when she started this race and when she stopped.

My husband, a funeral director, refers to death dates as
birth dates. I don't know if they're like first dates, or Friday-
night-at-the-movies dates—you know that movie that loops

through stages of sin and celebration, suffering and emancipation?

I do know this: it was left for me to discover, for *me* to see.
To stop in mid-stride, and recognize, in the splice of a moment,
that someone lived and breathed.

I stared at it and tried to discern what its finding meant, not
knowing I wouldn't know till the very next day—that Tuesday,
in September, that blue blue morning when all the world would run.

Aware of my watch and the seconds skipping, and my legs and lungs
saying go, go, go, I tucked the saint into my pocket, picked up my

head and continued to run.

BURIED

Henry scratches at my knees looking
for attention as I try to write.
I don't know where to start.
Time keeps me leashed

unwilling to let me roam through pages
of pain to find the beginning, and
figure out exactly when it was when
I discovered what forgiveness meant.

I don't know why it's necessary for me
to go backwards to find forwards
when I'm told —and I've known this—
that the past and future don't really exist.

Be in the now, be in the now!

But right now I say, tell that to Henry—
who remembers the history of every
bone he's ever buried in his little puppy life
his nose blackened with new mulch

and his tail wagging at his discovery:
Look at what I've got for you!
as if this is something new, and not planted by him,
not the thing he chose to inter

and sniff out when he was bored or lonely or
hungry or just wanting to chew, or discover.
I dislodge the bone from his mouth
all yucked up in saliva and gook and

throw it on the lawn with its pee stains
and mucked-up clay and patches needing seed.

He picks it up and heads into the garden.

THE DAY AFTER EPIPHANY

The day after you let me see You—
The whole of You—I got a migraine so
Debilitating I drove around Southampton
For two hours not understanding how to read
Street signs or decipher a map or even how
To vocalize the word "aspirin" at
The drive-through convenience store.

That *I* couldn't possibly be the one
Driving was not lost on me: I felt the split—
You taking the wheel and shepherding me
To the motel down the road from the beachhead
Where yesterday in the early hours a
Glint in the waves the size of a mustard seed
Became the entirety of the universe
And I had to shield my eyes and

Look at You in pieces—

The way I looked at the world today in
Zigzags, comforted by the belief
That my vision would soon clear.

NOBODY SAYS

Does anybody say to a soul just setting out
on its journey to the Planet Earth

that maybe that's not such a good idea?

Does the father soul say: "You'll suffer.
You'll experience severe loss and disappointment."

And the mother soul plead: "You're not
ready. Wait. Just a little longer. Please?"

Or do they kick you out, ready or not?

Does this young soul pick up its suitcase
containing whatever a soul would pack

(a set of sharp scissors to cut
that golden cord tethering it to Earth)

and be off on its way with
the mama soul clenching

the dishrag that is her heart and
the papa soul turning back to his

newspaper or his game and barely
looking up when he says,

"She'll be back."

BLUE

Henry prances after dead leaves
skipping along the cold pebbled walk.
He doesn't know dead.
He knows jump + sniff. He stares down cars +
marvels at departing planes.
He scampers + skips + trots + smiles
wagging his tail at the sun + the sky +
all that falls from it, dragging me
by the chain into the violet blue morning.

*   *   *

There was another blue. I've said it.
You know it. I watched that deep hue
from my pool, floating—after my run,
after I made my self stop watching the
replays of the towers that morning—my
arms spread like airplane wings, my body
weightless and the sky so still, everything
grounded and nothing grounded and
everything forever changed.

I resigned myself to the fact that I
wouldn't see my husband for years, he
making funeral arrangements for the
families and the firefighters after that.
Services for years and years, whenever
there was a new body part discovered or
a cancer named. Three dogs before Henry—

who doesn't know how much I still need
to be lead.

THORNY ACACIA

This I imagine—

Sprigs of acacia whipping in the desert wind
where He lives just below a rocky slope
leading down to the sea.

                        He must have known
the significance of the tree, the bush that burned
for hours without ever burning, this tree
that fortified the ark with two-by-fours
                      so man wouldn't sink.

He had listened to its stories as
He planed its bark for planks to make the table
He would sit at when He broke the bread—

gossip about the guard who'd cut off its branch
and forged it into a crown that would bloom even after
the sprig petrified and the tree died,

after the two-inch thorns crushed His skull
and released the tannins to ferment His blood
into the sweetest wine—

that pours out
                    from His side
on to this blessed earth,
                  Still.

TO PLANE

I think about the word plane
as my youngest sands the picnic
table, a task she takes on every
summer, earbuds in, goggles on, the
sander whizzing as it strips off
layers of stain.

A plane flies overhead. Biplane.
Some words and sounds put me into
other places, her planing wood,
the biplane planing the sky
mowing through layers of
space and time as

she orbits the surface, going
deeper into another place—another
plane—of existence beneath
the sawdust—banking and gliding
as the globe turns, her body
mirroring the motion in the sky.

HE BUILT THIS CITADEL

An architect sat at his drawing board with
a blank sheet of paper, and maybe he started

in the middle, or at the perimeter, or at
one of the lookout towers, thinking

about keeping people in or out, or protected,
or not, and perhaps this triggered something in him

something that happened to him as a child that he
hung on to and couldn't let go, not then, not now and so

that came out of his fingers, like in kindergarten, when he
drew a picture of his house and his family without faces:

stick figures, with ten fingers on each hand,
but no eyes, no mouths. And the house was gigantic,

so much bigger than the people, and the crayon was brick
red and he pressed down on it hard, so you could see the spot

where the point broke off and he needed to sharpen it.
And the windows had bars on them, or the panes just looked

like bars and if you looked really close you could see a face,
drawn very lightly in pencil, or a circle you could take

to be a face, looking out at the family who had walked away. [1]

<hr />

[1]   I remember building my own fortress. Graphed pages spread out on my
bed as if they were my favorite linens. Patterns of a house that would protect
& comfort me, and the family who lay inside. No one walked away. Even when
they needed to leave. When I needed to leave. Our breaths still soak its walls.

INKMAN

I wonder if the guy whose job it is
to fill this pen knows just how many words
or letters it can write before its ink
dries, or its slender barrel empties. Can
he calculate the total thoughts I'd need
to have, and does the quality of said
thoughts regulate the speed at which the ink
flows? Does my Inkman ever wonder, will
his Labor write of love or loss, of fear
or hate? And could emotion—in its most
fluid form—be transmuted, transferred, from head
to heart to hand to royal-blue ink spots
now bleeding through this crisp white page?
And what of my page?
Does my Muse consider it at all?
Its milkiness, its solid lines,
the empty spaces yearning to be filled?
So many of them, Inkman. So many blanks.

A SOLDIER'S WIFE
AT AN ANTI-WAR
DEMONSTRATION, 2004

I

Their boots are laid out in pairs, two by two
on the stark pavement in front of the federal building,
500 pairs of leather boots standing
in for each soldier killed in Iraq, boots
heel to heel on the cracked concrete, lined
in formation as they would have stood with
both legs, both feet, intact.

I look for your size among them, imagine
where you would stand now, here
in front of this edifice wrapped in a flag
full of lies. Dusty boots, so little worn,
lined up and going nowhere, singed laces tied
and bound together in a desert storm thick with
D-U-P-L-I-C-I-T-Y fingered in the sand.

II

"No weapons here, ma'am."

III

Your workboots still lie beside the door where you
left them that day, in the garage tinkering
with the engine, trying to steady your hands
as oil leaked into the spaces above your heart.

Does blood pool like that on the desert sand?

Because I couldn't imagine that parched, blood-sucking
earth leaving any evidence at all, not even a grainy kernel
of truth embedded in the nails of some kiss-ass journalist
catering to the masses at home with their popcorn

and beer, watching the war on TV. No, baby
the only evidence of anything at all

is the oil puddling on at my feet.

THE HEART POEMS I & II

I

The heart was a tube
before it chambered.

II

Sometimes when I'm lying on my side
sunken into the mattress like a ship sunk

into a great rift in the sea, I feel my heart
loosen from its spot in my chest, and crawl

like a slug, up my esophagus to the crook
of my throat—where it sits, pumping.

It doesn't want to be a tightly-held fist,
engorged. It wants to unfurl—

lay itself—flat—on my tongue.
Like before it was a tube. When it was

just flesh, embodied, just a tongue,
tasting life.

HEMINGWAY ON TOAST

Books surround us like creeping phlox,
vining through the walls of the new house,
piles leaning like Pisa.

"Just get rid of them!" You're sweating and
stumbling over the roots of stories I've packed
and unpacked—wait! how have you missed

this part of me?? The inked pages of my skin?
The way the spines of my books elongate me?
"Get rid of your books!"

Letters erupt from your lips, your body
feverish, rebelling as words sprout from your
skin. You don't know: *there is no ridding.*

When you sleep, I sneak off to faraway worlds,
enchanted rooms filled with dusty whispers and

tangled vines and writers quarreling in the dark.
Sometimes, I make them move just to stop the
grumbling—or start it: Hemingway next to Tolstoy,
Cather with Poe— books I intravenously read,

or give you for breakfast, scrambled and salted
between two slices of buttered bread.
Here dear, with your morning paper and coffee—

Hemingway on toast.

MAYBE, WITH VARIATIONS

Maybe I'll write this tomorrow.

I'll rise when the sun rises—assuming it will
rise—or rather, assuming the earth will turn
on its axis into the sun and maybe show
something of its self—as I will—when I write this
tomorrow, after morning meditation, after I count
my breaths, and pluck the clouds of
cotton from my brain, the covers off of a
sleepy sun.

Yes! I will write this with a clear head
tomorrow, after breakfast, after I juice my fruits and
veggies and cook my porridge—whole
grains, as a matter of fact. I'm taking the time to
notice things —like what I give my body and what
I don't— and so after I take care of it, and go
for my run because maybe it will rain and I hate running
in the rain, and after I walk the dogs—because, hey,

they need their exercise too, and after the bills are
paid and my mail answered and my library book read
because it's due back, and after I fix dinner and take
my daughter to dance—but before the sun sets, assuming

it will set, or assuming not at all because the sun doesn't
bounce up and down like a ball in the sky—and so assuming
the earth will make its rounds again as I will make my rounds,
then maybe

I'll write this right smack in the middle of one.

DEPTH

Sometime before she dies,
Aurora lay by the back door
watching slick sleet drill down
like rain—but slanted like this ////// ///// /////
forming acute angles with
the ground.

She tilts her Lhasa head,
mimicking the shape, and wondering
/// could she be? /// if the world itself
had suddenly slanted.

Watching her reminds me of
my own watching—alone,
from the 52nd floor of a condo
above Hell's Kitchen—forehead
pasted against a wet window,
wet eyes staring down at the rain,

noticing how huge raindrops are
at this height—how expansive and
filled—and I felt something within me
fill and something lighten.

I tried to follow the path of drops
speeding toward the city street,
trying to zero in on one or

two and failing—the drops dropping
too fast for my brain to process.
And yet, I saw how they morphed—

like this O > 0 > I I I > iiii
Gravity and velocity squeezing and
lengthening and forcing fluid into a
different form entirely. Me into

a different form. Sometimes, on these
occasions of sadness and noticing, I've
wondered what my dogs would think of
the world from such heights when for all
of their lives they've watched it from
the earth and never ever the sky.

Always, they'd contemplate the deep
blue from below, tilting their heads up
at a jet taking off or at the taunting of
the jays from the tops of the oaks, perhaps

even wondering // could they be? //
what it's like to fly or to look down
at the drops falling instead of
feeling them fall.

From the patio door, Aurora glances
back at me: *Stop thinking so hard.*

II

She's dead now. Years later a different
dog—Henry—moves with me as I move
from place to place, ground to sky—
and I wonder, does he know about
depth? And then I think, how silly
of me, this dog whose only sense
of the deep is to love and want love—
in its entirety.

We see the depths, but do we really?
We think we know form, but do we really?

I stand on astroturf at the dog park
looking up at my balcony and not
ten minutes later I'm up there looking
down at the ground trying to envision that overlap.
Trying to imagine myself being in two places
at once. Or two places of being.
Time an illusion, depth an illusion, love not.
Love is not. It fills my space if I let it.

Like this: I > OOOOOOO
Expansive drops of rain.

FIRST LOOK

My daughter globs on mascara before
first class, unaware of the hanging man
swinging beside her front porch.

When she's done screaming, she phones me:
        "Why, Mom? Why that tree? Why me?"
"Not you," I tell her. And then: "Why not you?"

She knows dead. She's seen the bloat of OD,
the bullet-bruised, peeled-back flap of
skin from the corpse her father has yet to embalm.

But never dead swinging, never the weight
of the pendulum ticking back and forth in
that prix fixe slice of time no one remembers ordering.

I don't know if she noticed—and she notices everything—
the way the wind might have nudged him or the putter
of squirrels scampering up and down the length of rope as it

swung, the same braided rope he clutched as he climbed
the embankment next to her college home. I see her
wet lashes, so long after the lengthening, those intense

blue eyes that always flicker. That night,
she didn't hear what she always feared she'd hear:
not heavy boots on crunchy leaves; not the grunts of a man

as he hefted himself up the second-tallest tree. For once,
she hadn't thought to be afraid. "Why didn't I hear him, Mom?"
Her breath slows as we talk about fear, about

intention, about being in a place of noticing.
Silence takes on a long, swaying rhythm and she is a child
again in my arms, rocking in the hammock in our yard.

It's hypnotic breathing together like that.

FIRST BREATH

I
Remember having gills?

Remember the rush of water flushing
through the slits in your neck
                as you swam, open-mouthed,
                through the algae plume?

And the slinky feel of protozoa clinging
fearlessly to the razored teeth in your throat,
                egging you on—
                faster, faster!

Remember the tickle of cilia
on your underbelly as you played
                hide-and-seek
                among the sea anemones?

Or racing with the shoal—
and the flutter of a thousand silvery fins
                as the pack danced to and fro
                in perfect synchronicity?

And remember, now, the lulling pulse of the salty sea womb—
its cradle-call from the deep; how you nibbled
                on its soft inner folds
                and drifted contentedly to sleep.

There you floated, impregnated with neither fear nor doubt,
nourished in the knowledge that what lives within is also without:
        that endless transmutation of self and sea,
        the universal soul at once set free!

II
But what of the vortex?
        The purge?

That siphoned the womb of its saline sea?—
A centrifugal force at the foot
        of existence, separating
        all that was from all still yet to be?

Oh, how you fought it!—
        thrashing about,
        alone and afraid, as it
        dragged you into its
        dark, drain-ed depths,

the saltless sea womb now shriveled,
        bereft,

its once-trusted walls clasping around you in a vise-like
grip; you, a fish trapped in a wormhole whose gills no longer flush
with sea life, whose marbled eyes constrict as you're pushed,
screaming, into a blinding light.

And you must choose now;
you must make that switch: Open
that other space within you, that space
that has been developing for you, unbeknownst to you, in spite of you:

        these two sacs,
        this delicate membrane,
        this point of transference,
        like water into wine.

Only water is air and air is blood and blood is food and food is life,
decaying, transforming, liberating life—just
as before, when you had gills, only
a little different—

        a displaced molecule
        or two.
        No big deal. Really.
        Water. Air.

        Remember?

Breathe.

FUNERAL FOR A FROG, 1970

Single file we tread
silently up the hill
like the ants we were then,
one-two, one-two, marching
hushed and determined
on a mound of brown grass
turning green.

Below, the little kids skip rope
on the cracked sidewalk,
singing merrily life is but
a dream and for a moment,
we stop and watch them play.

The sprinkler rotates: tick-a-
tick, tick-a-tick, to the tinny
roll of a drummer's beat,
tinkling over our sandaled
feet and splattering our

foreheads with an oiled water
oh so holy.

We blink as we pass, heads
high, hands clasped in reverie,
faces posed solemn and sad
like the ones on TV, watching
flag-draped coffins fade

into the static of a snowy screen.

We follow froths of petunias
and dry-mouthed impatiens, and
this time we don't look back.
Not at the row of mini-flags
muddied brown at the curb or
the oaks with their frayed yellow
ribbons flapping in the breeze.

We don't see the cars that come
and go, the black limousine.

We march past trumpet lilies
keening in the warm wind, their

rusty tufts of pollen hanging
by threads unseen, unaware
of the coming rain, or how
with a whisper and a soft blow
there would be nothing left to flower.

Had I looked up I would have
noticed a girl, like me, sitting
on the curb in her new black dress,
legs wide, fingers doodling in the
street sand, and nearby her family,
one-by-one sidling into the black
limousine. I would have seen

her palms pressing flat
against the tinted glass as if she could
leave this imprint, this part of her
here. With us. But I didn't.

I didn't see her at all.

At eight and newly communed,
I wore my tiara like
a high priestess, my white-gloved
hands cradling a small satin
prayer book, white cape swishing
behind me in the summer
sun, behind the pallbearer

who carried the shoebox to
the open grave dug between two yews.

You see, I forgot, it was her frog too.

BLANK CANVAS

I'm hunched over a blank page, my arms
spread out protectively around its edges
as if I were guarding my uneaten lunch,
when this teeny weeny spider plops down
right under my nose and sits there like it's
got some say in what I'm gonna write.

Well I'm not ceding ownership. Besides,
I'm God. I'll blow that little stinker off
the edge of Eden. Yeah, crush it with the end
of my unchewed eraser head before it shits on
my unblemished canvas.
And yet

here I stare, waiting to see what it will do
knowing at any point it could turn on me—
like that summer in my yard when I was
sitting at the bar—you know, writing?—and
this hairy little thing crawled along the
speckled granite and stopped.

Right in front of me.
It turned, stood up on its hind legs and
looked square in my face—I mean, eyeball to
eyeball, and I was curious, you know, thinking
wow this is cool— when I saw something in its
gaze and felt like I was already devoured.

So I moved. Quickly.
Just as it jumped on the arm of my chair—
which would have been *my* arm. Can I tell you
how pissed I was? How hurt?
Here I was giving it space to roam—to live!—
trying to make *contact* for Christ's sake—when

I could have easily taken its life away, flicked
it off that counter. Squashed it—splat—
with my new notebook, those empty pages.

But it didn't want its own space. It wanted
mine, my page, my life at a time when I just
wanted to close my eyes and let the pencil

roam, let it take the space before it would be
snatched away from me, before my life
would be taken away and every single page
would change.

And now,

I watch a hairy creature with skinny little legs
dance upon the white.

FLUID

Even the dog's nose runs.
A piece of fluid light I can paint.
And I think, now, about the viscousness
of color and if it can transmute the congealed
phlegm in my face into something
wonderful. Something more creative than

sickness. There are times when I step into
the canvas like it's an open door and I find
myself outside of myself. And so, so in.
Like the time I was grieving Aurora
and I couldn't heal, and I couldn't stop crying
about all I had lost every time I sat in the

Hemingway chair, each time I took out
my pen to write and she wasn't there
like she was for 11 years, her snout at the
sliding glass doors peering out while I
peered in, both of us noticing how something
grows and something always falters.

Finally I said, stop this. You are drowning.
And I was, the water born in me had
coagulated and there was no coughing it up.
And so I painted my beloved, her eyes human
eyes the kids said and I tried to change them
into dog eyes when my husband asked: "Why?"

I looked: All the light, the glistening
goodness I had painted in was blocked out and
I couldn't unearth the layers. All I could do
was paint again. And so with the tiniest of brushes
and a thick slime of white I went back to her eyes
again and again until I could feel her coming
out of the brush. Until I no longer held the brush
but was the brush and all its secretions.

And now here is Henry plastered next to me
on the bench in the yard on a fall
morning with split rays stroking the
crusted edges of the hostas on the side

fence. Henry, with his runny nose and eyes
secreting that white viscous goo, and

me in the midst of my own secretions,
thinking about the fluidity of
everything: ink, paint, snot, life.
Looking for elixir, Henry nibbles on the
grassy fronds by the pool.

I sip my green tea and taste honey.

THE HEART POEMS III & IV

III

At what point in our evolutionary history
did the heart become broken—

And at what point so easily repaired?

IV.

Do we really know our hearts?
        That dark place it sits inside?

Its valves, its canyons, the places of
        intersection and all those

spaces, all those cells
        needing to be filled?

I would like to be inside of myself.
        Float through those valves.

Feel how thin the walls.

I close my eyes and reach across the miles and
        feel my mother's heart as if it were

chambered inside of my chest.

I knew it first before my own heart started
         bleating.

Gestation 21 days. She was 21 years old.

Flesh to flesh, inside of the folds of her tissue.

Two organs playing. Two lives singing.

STILL WE PULSE

The embalmer wears the mask of
Anubus, the jackal-headed God
of the Dead. Behind him—

As he works, empty jars line
silty desert shelves, awaiting
a Life's ripened viscera.

Cavities are opened. Organs
siphoned without suture–
whole and swaddled in

linen strips––lungs, liver
spleen, all offerings from
this Life for life after we

drain. Each drop saved —
crucial for what we choose to
keep and choose to lose.

And what we think
needs to be contained.

Only the heart has no jar.

It cannot be unchambered or
disinfected or weighed or
mummified and Anubus longs

to hold it, to feel its pulse in
his palms.

And yet, he knows—
oh he knows— there is no
holding on. Still,

we pulse.

GUERNICA

Smoke burnishes from a bull's tail,
devil horns as white as the pale-faced
woman whose mouth hangs open in
anguish, a dead child cradled in her arms.

She beseeches the beast, pleading
the case of men—but what does it care?
Suffering is everywhere.
Severed limbs leap across a canvas,
black and white screaming out
to sharpened shades of gray.

Even the horse cries, riderless
under the blaring light of an evil
eye that sees all but understands
Nothing. No-thing. Not even what is
rooted into those linen fibers

Newsprint faded in the backdrop—
Erasure not possible. Can you see
The words? What do they say?
What would the artist say
—now—to the nations? His tapestry
no longer draped behind the
podium that once stood for peace.

Who is the beast?

YOU BURNED
MY FATHER'S FACE

Red raised welts—
road rage where he tries to smile.
Pieces of hair on his favorite couch.
And who knows what chemical fires

you set under his skin in claim of a cure—
          like you have that power—
you and that errant marauder, that mighty
Pyromaniac you concocted in your lab

for a fee. Quack! Did Death bribe you?
He on his dark Guernica horse screeching
into that golden bullhorn:
          Burn it all! Burn it all down!

My father sips his beer and watches his golf.
And you know he's just itching to crawl out of his
skin, and you know he's trying to believe every single
glowing ember of the hope you give.

I can't look at his face without biting my fist.

DONATION

What if love could be fed
intravenously?

Donated, like blood,
by people who love

who sit in donation mobiles
bloodletting on Lafumas

yukking it up with the nurse
who had pierced their veins with

just the right touch to get those
Love molecules moving.

See her fingering the tubes and
inspecting the fluid-filled bags?

See her packing up plasma in ice
for the labs and the hospitals and

the people who don't love or can't
love or just don't know how to love?

People depleted or whose bodies are too
exhausted to begin the process of

renewal and so they go in for their weekly or
daily dose and walk out with a smile that

radiates outward, their joy so eagerly shared.

SMALLNESS

I just saw a Matt Damon movie about an experimental
colony of small people, shrunken in response to
overpopulation and food shortages and the possibility of
extinction: Like little ants on a table and a bug so small
it looks like a speck.

But I wonder if we will make ourselves small because
that's just what we do to ourselves—
Not being enough.

And being like ants, replicating to be more. More than enough.
To make sure we're here for whatever it is we're here for.

Of course—there's the other end: We can make ourselves giants.
And be less. We can bully ourselves
into the universe and hover over everyone and everything
like a stalking president—or anyone struggling
with smallness.

We take in air—soap bubbles on a wand—
blowing up and blowing out until we pop and all that's left
are specks of spit and a belief of impotence and insignificance.

What we don't get is that we don't disappear—no matter how small or
large we are or were. There's that essence, you know. It's inside it's outside,

the border porous, and so so fine.

UNSEEN

A white cottony pall muffles

the sounds of the city street.

I can't see the ground but I know it's there;

there is that trust,

that compact between me and the pavement:

I agree to step gingerly upon it;

it agrees not to morph into a giant wormhole

and consume me.

The fog, by contrast, has no desire to negotiate.

It arrives as it pleases, with its secrets,

leaving me to guess

its intent.

REFRAIN

I'll kill you, you say.

Two inches from my nose
your words spittle your beard
red, coarse and holding on to
this pain you refuse to shave off.

I love you, Mom, you say.

The hairs stick out like pins and
I'm so captivated by your saliva—
how it clings and drips from the ends—
that I don't see your eyes splintering.

I'm sorry, you say,

not understanding the space I open
for you; what it takes to fully inflate
these lungs and exhale all those exhausting
years of forgiving just so you can occupy me

again. So often when you'd call, I'd sink
to the kitchen floor, needing the cold, hard
tile to anchor my thighs and keep me
from slipping into the vacuum of your rage.

I'll kill myself, you say.

This time I'm aware, as I watch your mouth move—
and *oh just to stroke that beard and the baby*
skin beneath it—that there might not be enough
of me left for you to smother. And I would let

you smother me if I knew you could find
release. But when I stare up into you, into
the heat of us, this space that is us,
this love slurping open and shut that is us,

I'm already gasping.

You need to go, I say.

Mom, you say.

                    Mom.

THE BEAN POLE

I can tell you where the hole opened
   And the hand reached through,
Jack snapping off petals He loves you
     He loves you not.

How we are drawn to beacons of blinking
   Green lights, on West Egg
     Eating ourselves out of our shells
Plucked really
   Did you hear the whoosh of His hand
    That jolly green

We exist for the purpose for sandwich
   We were born to die for and eat
    Wholly and fully those beans, us

(He likes the texture of edamame)

   Peas really, who survive perfectly formed
Under 20,000 leagues
  of Consciousness

To sprout

   For this hand that takes and this hand
   That breaks and this hand that
   emulsifies and this hand and this Hand and
   this hand that lets me be

So deliberately taken for you.

EXPANSION

I want to be a shape
in space.
I want to occupy vastness.
Triangulate my way through the cosmos.

The line I am veers off suddenly to the left
because it can.
Forms an angle like a crooked arm where a baby
lays her head into
something we can sink into.
Angles become squares.
Four walls and a threshold.
There is always a gate.
That leads into a wide open field
A field wide open for thought.

PINK-EYED MOTH, 2014

I

I'm at the picnic table—working through pages of hurt—
when I see my muse hanging on the table's lip.
I don't dare touch her.

Two eggs, lime green, cling to her bottom,
her wings fall leaves, camouflaged brown even
in summer; on them, two pink and black
"eyes" that seem to want to blink.

She clutches the wood, squeezing.
More eggs now. Still clinging.
Her front legs fold as if kneeling in prayer.
The eye-wings stare at me with knowing.

II

She's the sign I'd asked for this morning,
in my own kneeling. When I entered the yard
with my tears, there she stood, as if stuck,

on a spot on the deck with nowhere to hide.
So easily she could have died: stepped on
by me or the dogs. Snatched
by one of the crows.

I picked off a green leaf from the pear tree
whose leaves were always dying and
scooped her up and onto the table where
I could watch her and write. She let me.

Later, my pen paused exhausted after
flowing, I found her detached from the leaf.
A sticky paste remained, and with it, an egg
shaped like a tiny green tear.

III

There are four eggs now, and my lady's wings are
stretched like she wants to fly, but I think maybe
this is pain, that final push—she needing
the full space she can occupy to create.

She shifts her body and closes her wings
tight, as if they were just one wing; the bulge
of eggs beneath her growing. I count six now:
six eggs, six gelled spheres.

What's in me that I sit and watch a moth lay eggs?
God tells me to sit and see, and I listen.
But what do I learn? We all labor? We all have pain?

IV

This moth, my muse, my lady, will fly away
and leave her creations to live or die in the sun.
Either way an imprint, like eyes on a wing.

Her back faces me. I get up to find her face. Not
the wing eyes but her true eyes, the ones—
the one— that rested in me.

CRYSTALLINE

I've read that if you don't quickly wipe away
　　　your tears in space, crystals will form on
　　　　　the surface of your skin, sharp quartz-like
　　　shapes that would need some chiseling.

But who can chisel a tear?

And so I wonder, are all tears crystals?
　　　And crystals tears? All created
　　　　　with the same salt, the same vault
　　　of hurts?

When we finally become the next version of ourselves—
　　　this alien race—will we see this world
　　　　　through prisms? And remember what it is
　　　to taste a tear?

What tongue
　　　does the universe use to become aware of itself?

The newborn licks the salt of her mother's breast
　　　and thinks: *I am her.*
　　　　　She smells sweetness, and already feels
　　　loss. Finding she is not
　　　　　her Self but Something *other,* and asks:

—*What is this?*

Taste— her first sense after pain. And cold.
　　　Cold, pain, salt, and sweetness. This cost of hunger.

　　　—What are these sharp shapes emerging from these eyes?

The tear slides down and is tasted.

　　　*　　*　　*

If I could encapsulate my own tears into crystals—
　　　my first tear, and those I have created—

I would place each on the floor around me, ground myself
　　　and feel the air heavy with their weight—

stones circulating through my breath, through the swells
　　　of my heart and its heaving, through blood and bone and fiber

　　　　　and all this being,

these crystals I contain, myself salted and tasted
　　　dissolving now

　　　　　into sphere and space.

HAWK & SALAMANDER

Hawk grazes the burnished sky.
If it looks tentative it's because
the wind is tentative—
blowing hard, then giving up.
It's that kind of day.

The bird hovers, floats really, just above
where I lounge by my parents' pool—
with the old people and their noodles
bobbing up and down, smiling and tan.
Hawk scans the hot patio for food.

Salamander shrinks back into the garden,
its two front feet still plastered
on the concrete, two feet still in this
world while it stares at me, unblinking,
as if not wanting to miss what's right

in front of its face—
before it shifts. Before it takes that
evolutionary leap—like when it grew gills,
or found its legs, or discovered how to
change its skin. & Hawk, too, remembers

the heaviness of limbs, the weight
they carried and notices now the hush
and gust of wind and stretches out his
wings—to fly or float—it is that
kind of day. And here I am in it—

in the midst of noodles and white-
haired float and the tanned and the
smiling—remembering gills and
webbed feet. But not feathers.
Not wings. Not yet.

With my hawk eyes, I'm still searching
the sky, and with my little reptile
limbs, still hiding in the brush.

INFESTATION

I

My yard is super loud this morning:
crickets tree frogs beetles croaking
belching buzzing nyetting the sound
mowing across the lawn—a symphony of swarm.

If I were a bird, I'd be feasting, but none are about.
Not one. Like birds of sweet song can't stand
the biting tone of buzz and I get it: It's like

when my husband calls me from the car and the
seatbelt alarm keeps ding, ding, dinging or cable
news is blasting—how it drills into my ears; and
tanks my balance, so I can't soar. And maybe

that's it: the beetle's incessant chirping messes
with the bird's sonar, creating this forcefield
of noise, this tstststststststsssssssssssssss —

and you're either inside of it, or out.

We think we make this choice, but maybe
it's just the way we're wired.

II

I told my eco-organic pest company I'd cancel
my contract if they can't get rid of the
ants and beetles eating my oaks.

You should see the extreme trails they've
bulldozed from tree to tree, direct lines mapped
with a glaze that looks like liquid crystal.

I want to know: Why now? Why,
after 25 years of sharing the same space?

Before these were my oaks, they were woods
where we used to have keg parties, woods
that bordered horse trails, where the trees decided

who would live or die and thin themselves
out the way synapses in the brain snip away
branches of knowledge no longer in use.

I know it's all about self-preservation: trees need
to bring in the light; beetles and ants need
to feed on a life—but why

from the inside out? Why with those sharp,
discordant sounds that tear through the inner ear?

Henry's nose and ears are twitching, stinging
from the noise of the yard and the borders beyond:
a motorcycle, a freight train, a saw, a mower...

And then a jay—pissed off about something—
torpedoes in, and for a blitz of a second...

all sounds stop.

III

Blue, blue sky. Why blue only above? Why
not in front of my face? Why not a blue aura
around these fingers as I write?

My youngest comes out to the yard, still unsettled
by yesterday's "Beetles Incident" at Marshalls.
She was shopping when a special-needs man,
who had earlier greeted her with such joy—
    "Good Morning! Good Morning!"—
dumped a jar of beetles at her feet.
    "Can you step on these beetles?" he'd asked.
And she, backing away, said:
    "No, I'm sorry. No, I can't," and hurriedly
left to pay for her things. When she came home,
she was laughing, thinking she was pranked.

Today, she feels targeted:
  "Why did he pick me?" and then: "You know

it took me 23 years to realize The Beatles spelled their
name with an 'a'?"

Now I'm thinking about beetles and Beatles,
heat beetles swarming the yard, buzz-sawing
in one spot and then another with some kind of

symphonic coordination—or dis-cord-an-cy—
  She loves you, *yeah, yeah, yeah*—

I gaze at my daughter's beautiful face and absorb
her gentleness. She would have smiled at the man in
their "good mornings!" He would have sensed
her goodness, and trusted her to do this thing
    that confounded him.

"Maybe he found them crawling where he lives
and didn't know what to do," I offer. "Maybe, he
didn't want to, or couldn't, kill them himself.
They're different than ants or spiders—
    they crunch."

We talk about this difference in bugs.
How it's easier to kill some than others.
Easier an ant, harder a cricket—its guts splayed
all over the pavement, like discarded batter.

Does knowing about those insides give us pause?
Does it force us to think of it as a life? Force us to
stop the killing for a moment, or just leave it for
someone else—someone who doesn't mind the crunch?

She lifts her eyes, considering, the way she does
when I lay such things at her feet.
    "I mind," she says, and leaves me smiling
in the heat of the yard's symphony.

EMBEDDED

There's a fine line between mountain and space,
where horizon beckons with a magnetic finger and
draws me deeper into the summit of myself.

My strokes are even, steady—the brush so
light in my hand I don't feel like I'm painting—
or holding on to anything at all—like those times on

the trailhead when it felt like I wasn't walking—
when I was floating really, a cloud passing in the sky—
my stride so softly linking with my breath, and yet

so grounded—hiking poles scraping the ancient rock,
the worn dirt path, clicking like a metronome as I would
rise and fall and rise again.

And here I am, Lord—
staring straight into those snowy blue caps until
I am gazing straight out of them:

I am the Canvas.
I am the Blue.

THE MALLARD IN MY POOL

I watch you through closed doors,
my nose flat against the streaked
glass, wishing I had your grace,
wishing I could slip as easily
into the pool and glide so
elegantly in the torrent—
as if it were nothing.

What courage! Oh to stand so
stoically in the storm, unmoved
by the pounding rain, the heady
hiss of a strong soggy wind,
not a flounce in your feathers!

You turn to it as if it were
the summer sun—*hey there,*
Sunshine—your blue-green face
bathing in the brooding clouds,
the clackety clack of drops
nearly hard as hail but still
rain. Still steady streaming rain.

Oh, to plop myself in the midst
of it, knowing I could always
fly away! How I would strut and
swagger, naked in the squall,
wagging my tail feathers—
Look at me! So regal in the rain!

BETWEEN BREATHS, THESE TWO SELVES

The second I close my eyes,
You are here. The stillness
has invited you in.

Your presence envelops my
consciousness, sharing it as
if you were my sister
sharing a peanut butter
sandwich on the two-seated
swing in our backyard, there

we are, facing each other in a
deeply locked gaze, knees
touching, unshaven legs
pumping back and forth in
unplanned synchronicity.
A wind of many breaths whirls

playfully around us, my
sister's eyes glinting flecks of
gold beneath a summer sun,
years before the onset of
rust, our monkey bars shining
silver smooth and hot to the touch.

But still we touch. *Here.* Between
the spaces. You settle
into my mind, trying on
my ears, my nose, my eyes. Fine-
tuning the volume and
adjusting the lens until

I can't tell who sees or
who hears,
or touches.

A WORM IN SAVASANA, 2021

An earthworm stretches out on the concrete
and yawns, unaware of the crows pecking
in the grass nearby, hunting for
its kind of flesh.

    Does it hear their trilling?
Smell their need?
      That beaked hunger?

Or does it think that this moment of rest,
above ground, in the expanse of a summer morning,
with its blue sky and its moist sweetness
is worth the risk?

I am vigilant in my watching— from an old metal
rocker, white paint peeling off its sleeves—
blackbirds skirting my parents' yard like chickens
bobbing their heads looking for feed—

while the worm, in its blood-red blueness, peels itself
from the patio like Silly Putty, pebbled concrete
imprinted on its skin. It looks around, and once again,
lengthens.

    Why prostrate itself?
Is it unaware of the beaks? Or, uncaring?
      Is this a self sacrifice or a suicide?

It comes up out of the soil and into the bright,
and yet shades itself from singeing, bathing under
an old porous canopy my mother duct-taped
to four poles.

    It must desire this life.
    It must believe in its body. In its instinct and reflex,
    in the regeneration of holy flesh

and confident too, that it can be seen only by those
doing a certain kind of watching.

    *   *   *

I have to tell you: I don't know what became of it.

Later, I find my mother had dragged the iron chairs and the heavy glass
table around in a different direction. I knew then she had been thinking
about this all morning, the way she kept coming outside and staring as if
she were looking where I was looking but seeing something else unfold:
    How to sit. What to look at when sitting.

I would have told her: not how to sit but how to dive— deep
into a crevice and hide oneself in rocky stone.
I would have shown her how to wait, until evening, and rise up,
from darkness into blessed darkness.
    Into the fullness of embodied being—-

Stretching into Savasana
Into the light of stars.

TELL IT TO THE SKY, 2020

You think there's a membrane?
Tell that to the Sky, who breathes through the sheetrock and the
concrete foundation and the 1/4-inch window pane and the threshold
that holds the door you open and shut.

You think you open and shut?
Tell that to the mask that covers your face, not the cotton one but
the skin, the truth you conceal whenever you choose virus, or rage, or
judgment or shame.

You wonder why you see blue outside and not inside when the question
is: do I even know what blue is? How it seeps past the borders of this
world this body and how when you're on your back on the grass open to
the sky you are open to the sky.

Ask yourself: When I'm walking these strange streets am I loving on
the exhale? When our eyes meet and smile and we see that through our
masks do we ask, are we strangers?

Or do we feel the sky and the sun loving through it, so blinding in its
morning reach we forget for a moment who we think we are.

HOW TO FLATTEN, 2020

I have never seen a bird flatten itself until
I spied a sparrow slip through a slit in the eave
of Aunt Ginger's roof.

It wore a black mask around its eyes, like people do
around their fear-of-COVID faces, its feathers beautiful
shakes of black, gray, and green.

I wonder what it would be like to gracefully flatten. I say gracefully
because I know what it's like to be deflated, and this isn't that kind of
metaphor. This is about fitting into the sacred shape

of yourself—in this place, this universe, this eave that really needs you to be
a precise angle and line someone else can lean upon. Like when me and my
Uncle Johnnie built a house from a deck of cards and just

a whisper of wind—the door to the basement creaking, Grandma
calling—sending all those faces flying. And me, with my little-girl
nails bitten to the quick, scurrying to pick up the cards pasted on the
concrete floor, unable to lift them. And now,

I spy another sparrow becoming a card, and try my own becoming—
exhaling out all my air and feeling all my organs cave in, making a
c-curve of my body and not the one-dimensional aspect of who I want
to be—that singularity, that truth— and not what I am filled with: the
violence and noisy air of this world.

It's genius, really: in an eave, there's a nest away from the crows and their kind of blackness, one that requires a certain kind of shaping so you can sleep sweetly, and emerge into the bright blue morning, breasts puffed wide with air, awakening to your own voice singing.

THE CLAM

I swallow you whole.

Alive.

A conscious being, clinging to
 my soft flesh.

Witness to these inner
folds of me I'll never see.

Ours is a symbiotic love—

like the blue-green algae that
lives on your lips

You eat me, I eat you.
A mutual bounty.

But you know I need more.

So you surrender—
Slip into my brine.

THE UPSIDE OF DYEING YOUR OWN HAIR

The upside to hair loss is that when you dye your hair it
doesn't take as long as it used to.
The downside is cleaning out the drain.

I remember times in my life when I wanted to shave off
all of my hair, shed that mane that everyone coveted.
I just wanted to be a beautiful bald woman.

And now I'm older and wondering, am I still beautiful? —
these clumps falling out of my head, as if my brain can't
handle the pull of the root so busy it is doing all its thinking.

When I was thirty, I asked a famous author and playwright how
he decides what is a play and what is a story, and he replied,
"You'll know. Look at you with all that hair,

you have your whole life ahead of you. You'll know."
He didn't see the six-month bump of a belly in the darkened
auditorium. He didn't know I had three more lives at home, two

newly mine after marrying their father. He wouldn't see how
every day of this whole life I'd sit with my stories combing
through pages and struggling with shape and structure.

With the shape and structure of a life. I've never hid behind
my hair. Even when I wanted to hide. When I want to hide now.
There strands that refuse to be colored, that frame my face

just above the ears with a bloom of gray and white every time
I pull back my hair which is often. It's no wonder why
my body decided to pull back; revolt.

The upside of short hair is that you don't have to pull it back.
The downside is that you need to keep getting it cut.
The upside is that someone is always touching your head.

The downside is one day they will stop touching.

The upside of hair loss is that you are alerted with blaring sirens
that the medication you are on is just too much, that life has been
just too much. The downside is that it has been too much.

"We're just getting old," a longtime friend says. I smile at her effort
and think, not old, sick. The upside of being sick is that people
tell you they love you. They miraculously appear in your life.

They send you cards.

The downside is the feeling that I have been complicit in this.
My loneliness, my feelings of loss and despair have brought this on,
and my body, sensing a hello, opened these greetings of disease.

The upside of this realization is this revelation: There is still time
to stop suffering. Joy can occur at any moment I acknowledge it.
The downside is the gnawing feeling of lost time.

I squandered this whole life.

The upside of thinking about squandering a life is this reflection:
hair grows. It grows on my daughters, my sons, my grandchildren.
My dogs. Hair follicles are everywhere. In my ears. My nose.

I still see. I still smell

and in late hours of the night I still sweat. My bed wet, I feel hot
and cold and I remind myself of the upside: I am still alive.
And the downside: I'm still alive and I still don't know

what that means.

I wait for the dye to set and lather my hair into a thick foam.
I rinse, watching the water clear, even as my eyes burn.
I feel softness behind them. Ease. And in the mirror,

a smile.

SEA SKIN

Kayaking, I see the fascia of the sea
honeycombed shapes outlined in the sun,
        all heaving together, one kind of geometry.

Crystalline fractals lengthen and fatten as
        the sea swells into its sea skin,
and me with it, in it, wanting to paint it, still it,
        still these waves, be these waves

                        (I think of the meanings of "still": something
                                that is stopped or steadied; something
                        that ferments, fires.)

        These cells that can be all things, these
        waves I travel on, waves I can be.

                        ...
Looking down, in a shallow spot near the shore,

        the sand appears in ripples like the skin
around my knees. Aging, and yet fluid, my
        Self still fluid.

                        (Still = unchanged. How??
                                How can the sea not change me?)

The sea floor echoes the shape of its surface cells,
        like the myth that says what's below just reflects
what's above, but looking harder—trying to penetrate

        all those layers of looking, I see the ripples don't move.
Can't move. What looks like gently moving waves in sand is
        hardened. A rippled, wrinkled shell, aged and hardened.

        And I still (still = continuous) find—for a time—
rhythm in my paddling.

                    *   *   *

Here.

Rolling weaves of green.

Sea grass floating and wet blades flying
        each time I lift my oar.

Leaves of grass cover me, sticking to my bare legs
        as if needing something to hold.
And I let the fibers curl around my calves and

        hug me
until I am the one who is wet and rolling

and freed.

                    *   *   *

Once out of the sea weave, I pull in my paddle,

let my head fall back, face to the sky and its shimmering,
        my breath returning to its deep sea swell,
when a sound announces itself like a trumpeter,

            clearing his pipe of goo: a snort.
            Then: a snout. Then:
            a new shape in the sea: a manatee.

It blows its nose and gulps the air—and I clutch my
        oar, afraid and entranced and grateful. And look!
There! Its calf! Sauntering toward me as the sky rifts

            with the sea and its skin and its shapes and its
            song—and the sea cows graze on the floating fronds…

And here I am! Here I am, Lord, smiling
        my fascia stretching, these honeycombed cheeks.
The sun swelling behind them, and how can that be, Lord?

            How am I the one shining?

A LIGHT, UPON SITTING

A blue flame ignites
in the center of my universe,

a fiery silhouette behind my
eyelids, a furred patch of

Cosmic eye. It flickers as if
alighted from a candle's

wick,leaving me to wonder:
who struck the match?

or, if there was even
a match to be struck.

There was no apparent cause
for its ignition—

the flame just appeared
in my breath—

as if on some quantum level—
some God level—there was a

cause to effect: a cosmic thrust.
A holy wind whispering it into

existence.

Or maybe the flame
just wanted to be.

PRAISE POEM TO SELF

A Sound Poem from Turkana

Jackie! Here's to you, girl!
    To your Voice

        Once so stifled, so
        Afraid of its own sound

        Never saying, "No, no. No!
        This is not me!"

        Swallowed into submission
        Cowering deep in a bubbling gut

Here's to that Gut—to Guts!—
        To trusting Self and Sacred Song

Percolating Gut (thanks to Turkana coffee!)
Forcing Voice up. Out.
Exploding, Erupting

        A fucking Volcano. (Yes, go ahead, say it: Fuck.
        Your mother was forty before she said the word.)
        You talked about that recently—in your pajamas, sipping wine
        into the night—you talked about Voice
        about losing it and finding it

And what that meant (anti-malaria pills kicking in,
dipping in, nod to griot Bob
Holman, stay with it, Jack) what that means

Here's to you, girl—for embracing your special
Sound! For saying—No, for Shouting out:

Yes! Yes! Yes!

ACKNOWLEDGMENTS

Thank you to the following publications in which forms of these poems first appeared:

AbstractTV: "Between Breaths"

After the Pause: "Nobody Says"

The Big Muddy: "Maybe, with Variations"

BoomerLit: "First Breath"

CQ: California Quarterly: "Be Still"

Carbon Culture Review: "Inkman,"

The Cape Rock: "Thorny Acacia" and "Unseen."

The Coachella Review: "How to Flatten"

Doubly-Mad: "Sea Skin" and "Crystalline"

El Portal: "Depth," "Buried."

Euphony: "Praise Poem to Self"

The Evening Street Review: "Blue"

The Front Range Review: "The Heart Poems I & II," "The Heart Poems III & IV"

Glint: "Pink-Eyed Moth"

LitBreak: "Funeral for a Frog," "The Mallard in My Pool," "First Look," "The Clam," "Hawk & Salamander"

Mad River Review: "Slippery" and "Your Burned My Father's Face"

The NonConformist: "Embedded"

The Opiate: "Smallness"

The Round: "Autobiography," and "The Day After"

Prism Review: "Fluid"

Slant: "Air"

Streetlight Magazine: "To Plane"

The Summerset Review: "Donation"

The Umbrella Factory: "The Bean Pole," and "Still We Pulse"

Wayfarer Magazine: "A Worm in Savasana"

Whistling Shade: "Guernica"

For my parents,

for loving me.

A Special Thanks to
Stony Brook Southampton's
Creative Writing Program and Summer Conference,
especially to Julie Sheehan & Billy Collins,
In whose classes many of these poems were created.

ABOUT THE AUTHOR

Jacqueline Henry is a writer, poet, and creative whose work has been featured in numerous literary magazines and publications. Her poetry has earned critical recognition, including a Pushcart Prize nomination and first place in the *Writer's Digest* Poetry Awards for her poem "The Undertaker's Wife." Through her platform Faith-in-Form.com, Jackie blends her expertise as a Reiki Master, Somatic Life Coach, and certified Kundalini Yoga instructor to explore the intersection of writing and the healing arts. She holds an MFA in Creative Writing and an Advanced Certificate in the Teaching of Writing and Rhetoric from Stony Brook University—credentials that inform her holistic, embodied approach to self-expression. You can find her writing and reflections on Substack: reikiandwriting.substack.com